# CONTENTS

Title: Secrets of the Enchanted Forest: Unveiling the Mysteries of an Unforgettable Adventure

Author Megbo Beauty.

## Table of Content

# CHAPTER 1: THE CALL TO ADVENTURE

- Enigmatic signs and encounters that beckon protagonists into the enchanted forest

- Embracing the destiny that awaits and the power of self-belief

- Laying the groundwork for a trans formative quest

# CHAPTER 2: MYTHS AND LEGENDS: UNRAVELING THE SECRETS

- Ancient tales from mystical tomes: The origin story of the Enchanted Forest

- Unveiling enigmatic prophecies and unraveling their concealed meanings

- Encountering wise mentors who hold the key to unlocking the forest's secrets

# CHAPTER 3: FIERCE COMPANIONS AND UNLIKELY ALLIES

- Loyal companions accompanying our heroes on their perilous journey

- Mastering trust, collaboration, and embracing differences

- Discovering the concept of chosen families on the path to triumph

# CHAPTER 4: TRIALS AND TRIBULATIONS

- Overcoming a series of tests designed to challenge protagonists' character and resilience

- Confronting inner demons and conquering personal doubts

- Navigating treacherous landscapes and encounters with mythical creatures

# CHAPTER 5: UNEARTHING HIDDEN TREASURES

- Discovering mythical artifacts and powerful objects

- Learning to wield their magic for the greater good

- Deciphering ancient maps and riddles to unveil concealed troves of wisdom

# CHAPTER 6: THE ULTIMATE SHOWDOWN

- Confronting the primary antagonist threatening to plunge the enchanted forest into eternal darkness

- Harnessing newfound strengths to combat malevolent forces

- The epic battle that will determine the fate of the enchanted forest and its inhabitants

# CHAPTER 7: TRANSFORMATION AND SELF-DISCOVERY

- Protagonists' evolution from ordinary individuals to heroes of legend

- Embracing newfound strengths and talents

- Returning to the real world, forever changed by their enchanted forest experiences


Epilogue: The Legacy of the Enchanted Forest

- Reflections on the lessons learned and enduring bonds formed

- The impact of protagonists' experiences on their lives beyond the quest

- Encouragement for readers to embark on their own personal journeys of adventure and self-discovery

Introduction:

In "Secrets of the Enchanted Forest," bestselling author, Megbo B, takes readers on a spellbinding journey to a realm brimming with magic and mystery. Drawing inspiration from the highly coveted fantasy genre, Megbo B skillfully weaves an enthralling tale that transports readers into a world teeming with mythical creatures, hidden treasures, and life-altering quests. Prepare to embark on an unforgettable adventure, where ordinary individuals unearth extraordinary secrets, unlocking their true potential amidst the enchantment of the unknown.

"Secrets of the Enchanted Forest" is a mesmerizing tale of adventure, self-discovery, and the triumph of good over evil. Megbo B's captivating storytelling transports readers to a world where imagination knows no boundaries. This enchanting book invites readers to dream, believe in themselves, and embark on their own heroic odysseys. Be prepared to be entranced as you delve into the breathtaking realm of the Enchanted Forest, where secrets await and destinies unfold.

# CHAPTER 1: THE CALL TO ADVENTURE

As the first rays of sunlight parted the clouds, casting a golden glow over the quaint village of Oakshire, whispers of the enchanted forest filled the air. From the edge of town to the cozy cottages nestled in the heart of the village, something extraordinary was about to unfold.

Emily, a young and spirited artist, walked through Oakshire's bustling market square, the aroma of freshly baked bread and vibrant colors of the local produce dancing around her senses. But today, the village seemed different, as if it held a secret waiting to be discovered.

Enigmatic signs caught Emily's eye as she perused the market stalls. Images of mythical creatures and hidden treasure adorned each sign, leaving a mesmerizing imprint on her imagination. She couldn't shake the feeling that these signs were trying to tell her something, beckoning her to step beyond the borders of familiarity.

Curiosity coursed through her veins as she followed the signs, each one leading her deeper into the heart of the village. Whispers of a mysterious forest, shrouded in magic, grew louder with each step. A sense of destiny, unforeseen but undeniable, began to take hold.

Embracing the whispers and nudges of fate, Emily chose to believe in the power of her own potential. Doubts and fears lurked in the recesses of her mind, but a flicker of self-belief ignited within her heart. She knew that this journey into the enchanted forest would be transformative, challenging her in ways she couldn't yet fathom.

Pausing at the edge of the forest, Emily felt a hum of energy envelop her, tingling with anticipation. The forest's towering trees beckoned, their branches stretching like welcoming arms, inviting her to step into the unknown.

As she crossed the threshold into the enchanted forest, the air changed, crackling with magic and whispers of ancient wisdom. The sun's rays filtered through the dense canopy above, casting ethereal patterns on the forest floor. It seemed as though time stood still, suspended amidst an aura of enchantment.

Emily knew she had laid the groundwork for a profound and transformative quest. The signs, encounters, and her unwavering self-belief had brought her to this pivotal moment. Like a blank canvas yearning for strokes of vibrant paint, the forest awaited her touch, ready to reveal its secrets and challenge her in ways she had never imagined.

With every step deeper into the enchanted forest, a sense of purpose surged within Emily. She was not alone on this journey. Others had been called to embark on this adventure, their paths intersecting in extraordinary ways. Destiny had woven its threads, connecting their fates in a tapestry of friendship, courage, and the thirst for exploration.

As Emily ventured further, a glimmer of anticipation and uncertainty intermingled. She knew the road ahead would be treacherous and filled with trials to test her character, but she also felt a magnetic pull towards the wonders that awaited her. She was prepared to face the unknown, armed with nothing but her unwavering belief in herself and the power of her own spirit.

Little did she know that her journey had only just begun, and the enchanted forest held secrets beyond her wildest dreams. The call to adventure had awakened something deep within her, setting in motion a transformative quest that would forever alter the course of her life.

Within the enchanted forest's alluring embrace, Emily was ready to explore, to unravel the mysteries, and to discover the extraordinary wonders that awaited her. The call to adventure had been heeded, and she was prepared to embrace her destiny, forging her path through the realm of enchantment, one step at a time.

# CHAPTER 2: MYTHS AND LEGENDS: UNRAVELING THE SECRETS

Inside the depths of the enchanted forest, Emily found herself surrounded by an ethereal atmosphere, where the past and present intertwined. As she ventured further, the ancient myths and legends of the Enchanted Forest began to reveal themselves, whispering their stories through rustling leaves and murmuring streams.

With an insatiable curiosity, Emily sought out the tomes that held the secrets of the forest's origin. These mystical books, hidden away in an ancient library nestled at the heart of the forest, were said to possess the knowledge she sought. Once fragile and worn, the pages had weathered the passage of time, carrying the weight of countless stories within their creases.

As Emily delicately turned the pages, the tales of old unraveled before her eyes. She discovered the origin story of the Enchanted Forest, a realm born from the convergence of ancient magic and the dreams of its dwellers. According to the myth, the forest's creation was sparked by a celestial event, where a shooting star collided with an ancient tree, infusing it with extraordinary powers that transcended time.

Deep within those pages, she also came across enigmatic prophecies, written in cryptic verse and riddles, foretelling of a chosen one who would bring balance to the enchanted realm. Unraveling the concealed meanings within these prophecies became the key to understanding her purpose and unraveling the forest's secrets.

With determination, Emily searched for clues hidden within nature and sought the wisdom of the forest's wise mentors, the elusive beings who held the key to unlocking the ancient enigmas. These mentors, known only by whispers and legends, were said to possess ages of knowledge and insight, gifted by their close connection to the magic that permeated the Enchanted Forest.

Through her journeys, Emily encountered the first of these mentors, an enigmatic creature known as Alderheart. With antlers that reached towards the skies and eyes that shone with ancient wisdom, Alderheart seemed to embody the very essence of the forest itself. Guided by a profound sense of purpose, he revealed the path she must follow, leading her through meandering trails and hidden glens.

Under Alderheart's tutelage, Emily learned to decipher the signs and symbols that adorned the forest, uncovering their deeper meanings. He taught her to listen to the heartbeat of the forest, to recognize the subtle shifts in energy that hinted at the secrets locked within. Through their encounters, Emily's connection with the enchanted realm grew stronger, and the power of her own intuition became a guiding force.

As her knowledge deepened and her bond with the forest

strengthened, Emily encountered other wise mentors who shared their insights and stories. Each encounter brought her closer to understanding the mystique of the enchanted realm and her place within it. They spoke of forgotten tales, hidden treasures, and the delicate balance that must be maintained between magic and reality.

With every conversation and revelation, the forest unraveled its secrets, layer by layer, before Emily's eager eyes. The myths and legends that were once distant echoes became tangible truths, awakening a deep reverence within her soul. As she immersed herself in the forest's past, she began to connect the dots that would guide her toward her destiny.

Armed with ancient wisdom, newfound knowledge, and the guidance of her wise mentors, Emily stood poised on the precipice of her transformative quest. The secrets of the enchanted forest, once shrouded in mystery, were now within her grasp. With determination blazing in her heart, she prepared to delve even deeper into the realm's wonders, ready to uncover the truth that lay ahead.

# CHAPTER 3: FIERCE COMPANIONS AND UNLIKELY ALLIES

As Emily delved deeper into the enchanted forest, she found herself accompanied by a band of loyal companions, each with their own unique strengths and stories. Together, they would navigate the perils of their journey and unravel the mysteries that lay ahead.

One such companion was Aria, a fierce and agile warrior who possessed an uncanny ability to wield both sword and magic. With a fiery spirit and a heart full of determination, she became Emily's steadfast ally, always ready to defend her and lend her strength when needed. Through their trials and triumphs, Emily and Aria forged a bond that transcended their differences, learning to trust and rely on each other in the face of adversity.

Another member of their group was Leo, a mischievous yet resourceful rogue who knew the forest like the back of his hand. With his agile wit and cunning skills, Leo became their guide, leading them through the intricacies of the enchanted realm. While his carefree nature often clashed with Emily's cautious approach, their differences served as a catalyst for growth, teaching them the importance of collaboration and embracing diverse perspectives.

Among their companions was also Eira, a gentle and empathetic healer with a deep connection to nature. Through her quiet strength and nurturing spirit, Eira acted as the group's emotional compass, reminding them of the significance of kindness and compassion, even in the midst of great danger. Her presence served as a constant reminder that trust and love were just as essential to their journey as their skills and knowledge.

As Emily and her companions ventured deeper into the enchanted forest, they encountered various challenges and obstacles that tested their resolve. From treacherous creatures lurking in the shadows to unforeseen magical traps, the journey was fraught with danger. Yet, it was their unwavering unity that allowed them to overcome each trial they faced, standing united against the forces that sought to impede their progress.

Through their shared experiences, they discovered the concept of chosen families, a bond forged not by blood but by a shared purpose and the unwavering support they offered each other. In the face of adversity, Emily realized that true strength lies not only in individual prowess but also in the power of collective determination. Together, they created a tapestry of trust, reliance, and camaraderie that transcended the boundaries of their respective backgrounds.

As they continued their quest, Emily and her companions encountered other inhabitants of the enchanted forest, beings not initially perceived as allies. These chance encounters led to unlikely alliances that would prove crucial to their ultimate triumph. From mystical creatures and wise spirits to reclusive guardians, the forest revealed its hidden network of support and protection.

With each alliance formed, Emily and her group discovered the importance of embracing differences. They learned to look beyond outward appearances and preconceived notions, recognizing that the true nature of trust lay in accepting and understanding the unique qualities each individual brought to their shared journey. It was through embracing these differences that their alliances grew stronger, empowering them to overcome even the most formidable of challenges.

As their shared path unfolded, they realized that their journey extended beyond their quest. In the enchanted forest, they found a chosen family, individuals linked by a shared purpose and a bond that surpassed the boundaries of time and place. Through their trials and triumphs, they cultivated a deep love and connection, forging a familial bond that would remain with them long after their quest was complete.

In the next chapter, Emily and her newfound family would continue their journey, fueled by their unwavering determination and the guiding light of the forest's secrets. Little did they know that greater perils awaited them, and their unity would be tested like never before.

# CHAPTER 4: TRIALS AND TRIBULATIONS

As the sun rose in the enchanted forest, Emily and her chosen family prepared themselves for a series of daunting trials that awaited them. They knew that these tests would push them to their limits, challenging not only their physical strength but also their character and resilience.

The first trial came in the form of a labyrinth, a maze filled with twisting paths and deceptive illusions. It was designed to test their ability to overcome obstacles with clarity of mind. As they ventured deeper into the labyrinth, doubts began to creep into their hearts. The walls seemed to shift, whispering voices feeding their fears. But Emily, the group's guiding light, reminded them to trust in themselves and in each other.

Together, they navigated the labyrinth, relying on their instincts and the unwavering bond they had formed. In the face of darkness and uncertainty, they persevered, eventually emerging victorious. This trial taught them the importance of confronting their inner demons and conquering personal doubts, for it was their unwavering belief in themselves that would see them through the darkest of times.

As they made their way to the next trial, their path led them to a treacherous landscape filled with towering cliffs and raging rivers. The elements seemed to conspire against them, with gusts of wind threatening to blow them off course and torrents of water challenging their every step. It was in this moment that they realized the true extent of their physical resilience.

With Eira's healing touch and Leo's nimble agility, they navigated the perilous terrain, inching closer to their goal. Aria's unwavering strength and Emily's unwavering determination propelled them forward. They discovered that in the face of danger, their individual strengths complemented one another, creating a formidable force that defied the odds.

However, it was not just the landscape that tested their endurance. Along their journey, they encountered mythical creatures, whose power and cunning were legendary. From fire-breathing dragons to cunning sphinxes, each encounter demanded not only physical prowess but also quick wit and strategic thinking.

The dragons, with their scales gleaming like molten gold, challenged the group to outwit them in a battle of intellect. Through a series of riddles and puzzles, the group had to unravel the mysteries presented to them. It was in this trial that Leo's sharp mind and Aria's resourcefulness shone brightly, solving the riddles with ease.

Facing sphinxes proved to be an entirely different challenge. With their captivating gaze and riddles that tested the very fabric of their beliefs, the sphinxes forced Emily and her companions to confront their values and question their sense of self. Each riddle carried a lesson, challenging them to reevaluate their purpose, motivations, and the choices they had made thus far.

In the face of each trial, the group grew stronger and more resolute. They discovered depths of themselves they never knew existed and triumphed not just over external obstacles but their own limitations as well. These trials were not simply tasks to overcome; they were transformative experiences that molded them into the heroes they were destined to become.

As they emerged from the trials, battered yet victorious, Emily and her chosen family found themselves united in their shared resilience and unyielding determination. The path ahead remained uncertain, and greater perils still awaited them in the heart of the enchanted forest. But armed with their newfound strength and the unbreakable bonds they had forged, they were ready to face whatever challenges lay ahead in their quest for triumph and salvation.

In the next chapter, Emily and her companions would venture deeper into the mystical forest, where ancient secrets and untold dangers awaited them. They would uncover forgotten histories, confront powerful adversaries, and discover the true extent of their destinies. The trials they had overcome were only the beginning, for the enchanted forest held far greater tests of their mettle.

# CHAPTER 5: UNEARTHING HIDDEN TREASURES

As the heroes ventured deeper into the mystical forest, their hearts filled with a sense of anticipation and wonder. They knew that within the heart of the enchanted forest lay hidden treasures and mythical artifacts, each holding the key to unlocking their true potential. With newfound strength and a burning desire to fulfill their destinies, Emily and her chosen family embarked on a quest to seek out these powerful objects.

Their journey led them to a clearing in the forest, where an ancient tree stood tall and majestic, adorned with shimmering crystals and luminescent markings. It was said that within this sacred tree resided a collection of mythical artifacts, each possessing a unique power. As they approached, a soft voice echoed in their minds, revealing the daunting challenge that lay ahead.

To earn these prized artifacts, they would have to prove not only their worthiness but also their ability to wield their magic for the greater good. The tree offered them a series of trials, each designed to test their magical abilities and harness their inner strength. They had to master control over the elements, summoning fire, water, earth, and air with precision and purpose.

Through seemingly insurmountable challenges, Emily and her companions discovered the depths of their magical abilities. Leo, with his affinity for fire, ignited his passion and directed flames with unwavering focus. Aria, connected to the water element, harnessed her emotions and manipulated waves with grace and ease. Eira, attuned to the earth, commanded the very ground beneath her, shaping and molding it to her will. And Emily, bearing the power of the air, rode invisible currents, unleashing gusts and gales that swept away obstacles.

In the wake of their successes, they were granted access to the sacred tree's hidden chamber. There, they found a vast collection of ancient maps and riddles, each leading to concealed troves of wisdom scattered throughout the enchanted forest. It was through the deciphering of these maps and riddles that they would gain invaluable knowledge about their past and the grand tapestry of their destiny.

With the maps clutched in their hands and the riddles burning in their minds, the heroes embarked on a new phase of their journey. They trekked through dense undergrowth, climbed towering peaks, and traversed treacherous ravines, following the cryptic directions bestowed upon them. Along the way, they encountered mythical creatures that guarded the secrets of the forest, testing their resolve and challenging their mastery of both magic and intellect.

Each riddle they solved and each map they followed brought them closer to unearthing hidden treasures. These treasures were not just material wealth but also portals into realms of profound wisdom and timeless knowledge. The heroes would unearth ancient scrolls inscribed with forgotten languages and encounter mystical artifacts that held the power to shape destinies.

In their pursuit of these treasures, the heroes discovered that it was not just the acquisition of power that mattered but also how they used it. They learned that the true value of these artifacts lay in their ability to bring about positive change, to heal the wounded, and to protect what was sacred. They were now entrusted with artifacts that had the potential to unleash both creation and destruction, and it was their responsibility to ensure that they were wielded wisely.

With newfound magical prowess and an abundance of ancient wisdom, Emily and her chosen family continued to journey deeper into the enchanted forest. They knew that the trials they had conquered and the treasures they had found were only part of a greater tapestry of their destiny. The path ahead was still filled with uncertainties and dangers, but they were prepared to face whatever challenges lay in wait, armed with their powers and a deep understanding of the responsibilities that came with it.

In the next chapter, the heroes would confront powerful adversaries who sought to exploit the forest's secrets. They would face tests of loyalty, confront their deepest fears, and forge alliances with unlikely allies. The discoveries and revelations that awaited them would reshape not only their perception of the enchanted forest but also their perception of themselves. And through it all, their bond as a chosen family would grow stronger, united by a shared purpose and an unyielding determination to bring light to the shadows that threatened their world.

# CHAPTER 6:
# THE ULTIMATE
# SHOWDOWN

As Emily and her chosen family ventured deeper into the enchanted forest, the sense of impending doom hung heavy in the air. They had learned of a malevolent force, an ancient antagonist who sought to plunge the forest into eternal darkness. It was a being of immense power, capable of obliterating everything in its path. Their journey had led them to this moment—the ultimate showdown that would determine the fate of the enchanted forest and all who called it home.

Led by a vision, the heroes arrived at the heart of the forest, where a great shadow loomed over the land. The primary antagonist stood before them, emanating an aura of darkness that seemed to engulf everything around it. Its eyes glowed with malevolence, reflecting the centuries of darkness it had embraced.

In this climactic battle, the heroes would have to harness their newfound strengths and master the lessons they had learned throughout their journey. Each had grown exponentially, understanding the intricacies of their magic and the power they held within. Their abilities had merged with their beings, becoming extensions of their very essence.

Emily, who had always been boundless in her empathy and compassion, was now a beacon of light, emanating warmth and hope. Her adversaries recoiled in the face of her unwavering spirit, for she understood the strength that lay in kindness and forgiveness. Her aura of light repelled the darkness, exposing the true nature of their enemy.

Leo, whose fiery determination had guided him through countless trials, now manifested his inner flame into a blazing inferno. With each flick of his wrist, cascading streams of fire engulfed the antagonist, tearing through its defenses. The scorching flames sang a symphony of justice, ridding the forest of the malevolent presence.

Aria, with her deep connection to water, harnessed the fluidity and adaptability of her element. In the midst of battle, she conjured tidal waves, crashing against the antagonist with an unstoppable force. The water surged with power, purifying all it touched, washing away the darkness it had brought.

Eira, attuned to the earth's heartbeat, summoned a seismic strength that shook the very foundations of the forest. She manipulated the terrain, creating towering walls and impenetrable barriers to protect her allies. Her connection with nature imbued her with the resilience needed to withstand even the harshest assault.

Together, the heroes launched an assault on the primary antagonist, their combined strength forming an unyielding force against the encroaching darkness. Power clashed with power, the clash of magic reverberating through the forest, reaching every inhabitant who held their breath in anticipation.

The battle raged on, each hero unleashing their most powerful spells and abilities. The enchanted forest bore witness to an epic clash that would determine the fate of all who called it home. The stakes were unimaginable, for if the antagonist prevailed, the forest's magic would wither away, leaving its inhabitants consumed by eternal gloom.

The forest seemed to hold its breath as the heroes pushed through their limits, determined to protect not just their chosen family but also the delicate balance of light and dark that had sustained the enchanted forest for centuries. With each blow, they chipped away at the antagonist's defenses, leaving nothing but vulnerability in its wake.

In a final surge of strength, the heroes combined their powers, forming an intricate dance of elemental forces. The light, fire, water, and earth melded into a tornado of energy, enveloping the antagonist in an all-encompassing vortex. It struggled against the onslaught but ultimately succumbed to the overwhelming power of unity and purpose.

As the darkness dissipated into nothingness, the enchanted forest breathed a sigh of relief. The threat that had loomed over the land had been vanquished, and the heroes stood triumphant. The inhabitants of the forest emerged from their hiding places, singing songs of gratitude and celebrating the return of light and hope.

Emily and her chosen family had not only saved the enchanted forest but also cemented their place in its history. They had learned that true power lay not in destruction but in the ability to protect and restore. Their journey had transformed them from mere individuals into a collective force of nature, capable of withstanding any challenge that threatened their world.

With a renewed sense of purpose and immense gratitude, the heroes bid farewell to the enchanted forest. They carried with them the memories of the battles won, the wisdom they had gained, and the unyielding bond forged amidst adversity. Their journey was far from over, but they walked away with a profound understanding that their united strength could conquer any darkness that dared to encroach upon their home.

In the next chapter, new horizons awaited the heroes as they turned toward the vast unknown. Their experiences in the enchanted forest had prepared them for the challenges that lay beyond these enchanted borders, where new alliances would be formed and hidden treasures would be uncovered. And as they ventured forth, they carried the lessons of their past, ready to face whatever awaited them on their continuing quest for a brighter future.

# CHAPTER 7: TRANSFORMATION AND SELF-DISCOVERY

As Emily and her chosen family bid farewell to the enchanted forest, they embarked on a journey back to the real world, forever changed by their experiences. They had transformed from ordinary individuals into heroes of legend, armed with newfound strengths and talents that would shape their lives from this point forward.

The path back was not easy, for the enchanted forest had left an indelible mark on each of them. They found themselves grappling with a mix of emotions—gratitude for their triumphs, nostalgia for the magical world they had left behind, and excitement for the possibilities that awaited them in their own reality.

Upon returning, they noticed that their transformation was not only evident in their hearts and minds but also physically manifested. Emily discovered that her once chestnut hair now shone with threads of shimmering silver, a reflection of the enduring light she had carried within her. Leo's eyes, once an ordinary brown, were now a mesmerizing shade of amber, mirroring the fire that had fueled his determination. Aria found that her fingertips glowed with a soft, ethereal blue, a testament to her affinity for water that could not be extinguished. And

Eira, as she stepped on familiar ground, realized that every step she took seemed to resonate with the earth beneath her feet, a connection that would never waver.

Though the physical changes were surprising, they embraced them as reminders of the incredible journey they had embarked upon and the powers they wielded within. They understood that their journey had been as much about self-discovery as it had been about saving the enchanted forest.

Back in the real world, the heroes faced new challenges. They had to find a way to reintegrate into society while carrying the weight of their experiences and transformations. At times, they felt like they were living in two worlds—simultaneously existing in the ordinary realm and being forever connected to the enchanted forest that had become their home.

Yet, with each passing day, they discovered that their newfound strengths and talents were not confined to the boundaries of the enchanted forest. Emily's empathy and warmth brought light to those she encountered, inspiring acts of kindness and fostering connections. Leo's determination and passion ignited his pursuits, propelling him towards success in areas he had never dreamed possible. Aria's affinity for water led her to a career in marine biology, where she played a crucial role in conserving the fragile ecosystems of the oceans. Eira's connection to the earth guided her towards sustainable agriculture, where she shared her knowledge with others, nurturing not only the land but also the souls of those she touched.

Through their courage and resilience, they inspired others to tap into their own hidden strengths and talents, promoting the idea that everyone possesses the power to change the world in their own unique way. They started a movement that rippled through their communities, reminding people that there was magic in embracing who they truly were.

The heroes often found solace in gathering together, sharing stories of their adventures in the enchanted forest, and reminiscing about the battles they had won and the friendships they had formed. These moments of connection reminded them that their chosen family extended beyond the borders of either realm. They were bound by something much deeper—a shared journey of self-discovery and transformation.

As time passed, their experiences in the enchanted forest became the foundation for a new chapter in their lives. They not only carried the memories in their hearts but also used their newfound strengths and talents to shape the world around them. They realized that the enchanted forest had been a catalyst for their evolution, and they were determined to honor that transformation by making a difference in their world.

In the closing pages of this chapter, the heroes understood that their journey of self-discovery was far from over. They had become beacons of hope, urging others to embrace their own unique paths and unlock their hidden potentials. They walked forward, knowing that each day held the potential for new adventures and challenges, ready to face the world with open hearts and minds, forever changed by their enchanted forest experiences.

Epilogue: The Legacy of the Enchanted Forest

As the heroes looked back on their journey through the enchanted forest, they couldn't help but be overwhelmed by the lessons they had learned and the enduring bonds they had formed. The impact of their experiences extended far beyond the confines of the quest itself, leaving an imprint on their lives that would guide their choices for years to come.

The enchanted forest had taught them the power of unity and friendship, highlighting the significance of having a chosen family who shared their dreams and fought alongside them. They understood that true strength was not just in individual abilities, but in the collective support they garnered from each other. The bonds forged in the face of adversity were unbreakable, and they knew they could rely on their companions, no matter where their paths led.

More importantly, the heroes had discovered the importance of embracing one's true self and the strengths that lay within. The enchanted forest had served as a mirror, reflecting their innermost desires, fears, and potential. It had pushed them beyond their comfort zones and forced them to confront their own limitations. Through this, they realized that the true magic was not in being someone else, but in accepting and embracing their own unique qualities.

Their experiences in the enchanted forest had also taught them the value of perseverance and resilience. They had faced countless challenges and obstacles, but they had never lost sight of their purpose. In the face of adversity, they found the strength to push forward, to stand tall in the face of darkness, and to never abandon hope. Their unwavering determination had not only saved the enchanted forest but had also shown them the immense power that lies within the human spirit.

Beyond the quest, the impact of their experiences continued to shape their lives. Each of them had discovered their true passions and talents, using them as weapons of positive change in the world. Emily became a renowned therapist, helping others find their own paths to self-discovery and healing. Leo, fueled by the fire within him, became an advocate for social justice, using his voice to fight for fairness and equality. Aria's love for water led her to become a revered environmental activist, spreading awareness about the importance of preserving our planet's precious resources. Eira, guided by her bond with the earth, became a pioneering force in sustainable architecture, weaving together nature and design to create harmonious living spaces.

The heroes knew that their time in the enchanted forest had bestowed upon them a great responsibility—to carry the lessons learned and the magic experienced into the world. They resolved to be beacons of inspiration, encouraging others to embark on their own personal journeys of adventure and self-discovery. They created a foundation, dedicated to supporting those seeking transformation and providing resources for those ready to embark on quests of their own.

In the closing of their story, the heroes turned to the readers, imploring them to discover the magic that lies within themselves. They emphasized that while the enchanted forest may be fictional, the transformative power of self-discovery and adventure was very much within reach. They invited readers to take the first step towards their own quests, encouraging them to explore their passions, face their fears, and embrace their true selves.

The legacy of the enchanted forest lived on not only through the heroes but also through those inspired by their journey. Their tale became an eternal reminder that life is a constant adventure, and that within each person lies the potential to create their own magical stories of growth and self-discovery.

As the final page closed, the readers were left with a sense of empowerment and a burning desire to embark upon their own personal quests. They understood that the journey would not always be easy, but that the rewards of self-discovery were immeasurable. Inspired by the heroes' legacy, they would go forth, ready to create their own tales of transformation, leaving their own marks on the world.

And so, the story of the heroes, the enchanted forest, and the power of self-discovery continued to resonate, offering hope and inspiration for generations to come.